All About Me

By Margaret Clyne

Contents

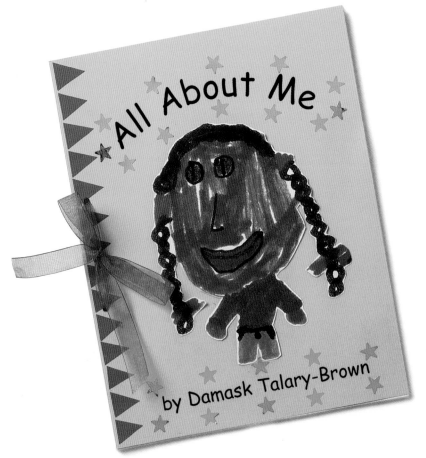

2

What You Need

- card
- a hole puncher
- ribbon
- pencils
- crayons
- marker pens
- scissors
- glue
- stickers
- photographs

Make a book that's all about you!
Write and draw things you like. Add
stickers and photographs, too. Use the
ideas inside or add your own. Fill as many
pages as you need to make your book.

Get Started

First, choose two sheets of card. Punch
holes down the left side of each sheet.
These will be the covers of your book.

Ideas

- your photo
- a drawing of yourself
- your artwork
- your handprints
- stickers

Write the book title on the front cover. Next, add the author's name. That's you! Decorate the cover.

Write About Yourself

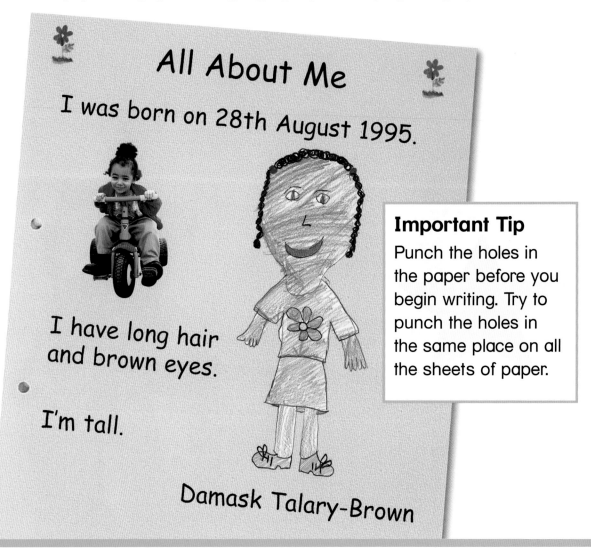

All About Me

I was born on 28th August 1995.

I have long hair and brown eyes.

I'm tall.

Damask Talary-Brown

Important Tip

Punch the holes in the paper before you begin writing. Try to punch the holes in the same place on all the sheets of paper.

Now write about yourself. Take a new sheet of paper. What do you look like? Are you tall or short? Add a picture of yourself, too. Write your name.

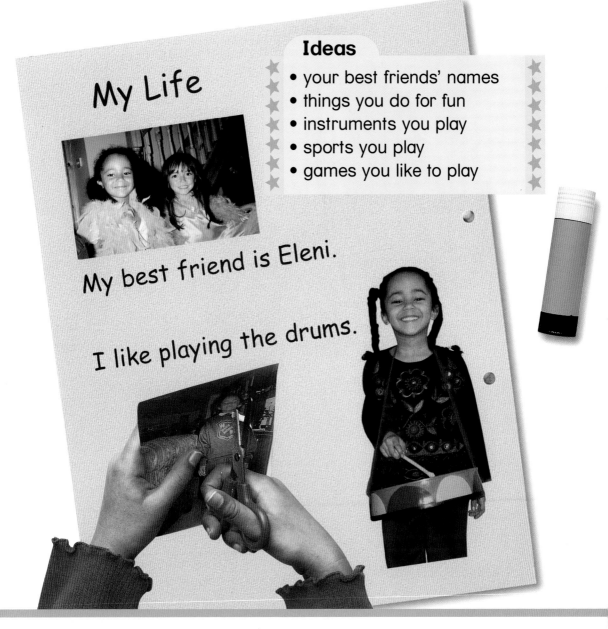

My Life

Ideas
- your best friends' names
- things you do for fun
- instruments you play
- sports you play
- games you like to play

My best friend is Eleni.

I like playing the drums.

Write about your life. Do you have a hobby? Do you play sports? Write about how you like to spend your time.

My Favourite Things

I like red.

I like painting.

Ideas
- favourite colour
- favourite game
- favourite book
- favourite foods
- favourite animal
- favourite places

I like swimming.

Next, add a page about your favourite things. You can write about things you don't like, too. Don't forget to decorate your page.

8

Special Things

I wish I could fly.

I want to travel around the world.

Being by the sea makes me happy.

Ideas
- what you want to be when you grow up
- how you would change the world
- crazy dreams you've had
- what makes you happy and sad

What are your dreams for yourself?

If you had three wishes, what would they be?

What other special thoughts do you have?

Write about them on the back of the page.

9

Make a Timeline

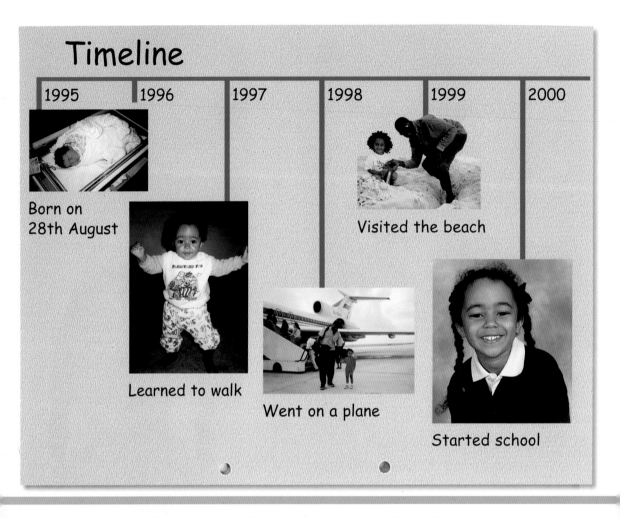

Timeline

| 1995 | 1996 | 1997 | 1998 | 1999 | 2000 |

Born on
28th August

Learned to walk

Went on a plane

Visited the beach

Started school

Now make a timeline for your book. Turn
a sheet of paper sideways. The holes should
be at the bottom of the page. Draw a line
at the top of the page. Then write down
important times in your life.

Ideas

- when you took your first steps
- when you learned something special
- when you went to school
- when you went on a trip

If you don't know what to write, ask your family. Talk about things that you did when you were little. Look at family photographs for ideas. Choose your favourite photographs for your timeline.

11

Write About Your Family

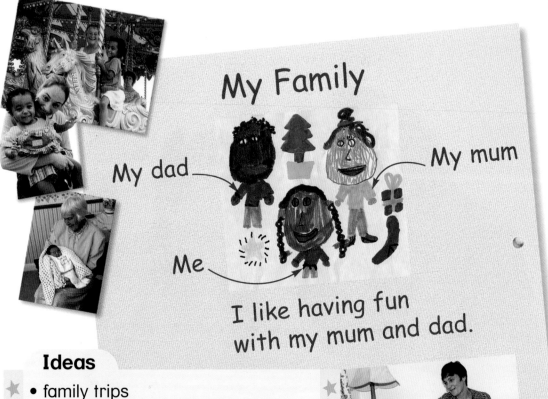

My Family

My dad

My mum

Me

I like having fun
with my mum and dad.

Ideas
- family trips
- five things you like about
  your family
- special things people do and say
- your family tree

On the next page write about your family.
Write their names and add drawings
of them. Write about things you like
to do together, too.

My Pet

I like giraffes.

I would like to have a horse.

Do you have an interesting pet? Do you want one some day? What do you like about your pet? Maybe your pet deserves its own page.

Write About Your Neighbourhood

Park

My street

My house

My school

Shops

Write about where you live. What is your neighbourhood like? Draw a map of your neighbourhood. Show special places, like parks and shops.

Put It All Together

Important Tip
When you put the
pages together, keep
the punched holes
on the left side.

All About Me

by Damask Talary-Brown

Last put your book together. First, put all
the pages in order. Then add the covers.
Finally, tie the book together with ribbon.
Now you can share your book.

16

Next, draw your home. You can draw your school, too. Take photographs of things in your neighbourhood. Then stick them onto the page.

This is my home.
It has a garage on the side.

My room

In the park

Ideas

- neighbourhood photographs
- five great places in your neighbourhood
- a list of neighbourhood sounds
- photographs or drawings of people in the neighbourhood